5-28-2013   H.R.

MOUNT OF COMMUNION

Mount Angel Abbey
1882–1982

Mount of Communion: Mount Angel Abbey 1882–1982
Copyright © 1982
Revised Edition Copyright © 1985
Second Revised Edition Copyright © 2012 by
Mount Angel Abbey, St. Benedict, Oregon U.S.A.

Printed in the United States of America

Revised Edition Credits:
Edited by Br. Neil Yocom, O.S.B.
Text by Fr. Martin Pollard, O.S.B. and Fr. Hugh Feiss, O.S.B.
Captions by Br. Neil Yocom, O.S.B. and Fr. Martin Pollard, O.S.B.
Photographs from the Mount Angel Abbey Archives with additional photography by Fr. Remi Shibler, O.S.B.;
Br. Benjamin Degnin, O.S.B.; Br. Neil Yocom, O.S.B. and Vince Zollner
Cover Art by Br. Claude Lane, O.S.B.
Typesetting by Carol Sanne
Printed by Capital City Graphics, Salem, Oregon.
Special thanks to Fr. Ignatius Groeger, O.S.B.; Fr. Augustine DeNoble, O.S.B.; and Fr. Philip Waibel, O.S.B.
Also, thanks to Fr. Prior Peter Eberle, O.S.B.; Fr. Albert Bauman, O.S.B.; Fr. Paschal Cheline, O.S.B.;
Br. Jerome Young, O.S.B. and Br. Nathan Zodrow, O.S.B.

Second Revised Edition Credits:
Edited by Fr. Augustine DeNoble, O.S.B.
Text by Fr. Martin Pollard, O.S.B. and Fr. Hugh Feiss, O.S.B.
Captions by Br. Neil Yocom, O.S.B., Fr. Martin Pollard, O.S.B., and Br. Cyril Drnjevic, O.S.B.
Photographs from the Mount Angel Abbey Archives with additional photography by Br. Cyril Drnjevic, O.S.B.
and Novice Jackson Conocido.

Contents

Introduction. v
1. 1882–1892. 1
2. 1892–1910. 15
3. 1910–1930. 30
4. 1930–1950. 48
5. 1950–1974. 56
6. 1974–1982. 72
Map of Hilltop. 87
Historical Chart. 88

INTRODUCTION

In Central Italy, sometime in the first half of the sixth century, an abbot, known to posterity as St. Benedict, wrote down his rule for monks. By that time Christian monasticism had been developing for over two hundred years. Christian monks had written many books of maxims, rules, and theology, explaining their way of life as hermits or as monks and nuns living in community. St. Benedict was familiar with this earlier monastic tradition. With a discerning eye he selected the ideas and regulations which he wished to retain; then he wove these into a rule which was destined to have an enormous influence in the history of Western Christianity.

According to Benedict's Rule, when a novice has completed his probationary period in the monastery, "he comes before the whole community in the oratory and promises stability, fidelity to monastic life, and obedience" (Rule of Benedict, ch. 58). The obedience that the novice promises is to rule, abbot and community, but ultimately to Christ. Benedict's idea of stability extends the Desert Fathers' prohibitions against wandering into a lifelong attachment of the monk to the place and people of his community. The promise of fidelity to monastic life is a commitment to pursue the goal of Christian monasticism—a Spirit-inspired life of Christian love in the presence of God the Father—and to use the monastic means to this goal: celibacy, simplicity, holy reading, hospitality, community work, and prayer.

The history of any monastic community will be the history of a place—chosen, cultivated, hallowed and fashioned by the community. It will be the history, too, of an obedience—a tradition, a rule, an abbot, a community. This obedience has nothing to do with absolutism; it is not reducible to efficiency and good order; it does not exclude conflict and controversy. This obedience is an attempt to follow wholeheartedly the Rule of Benedict's opening admonition, "Listen carefully, my son, to the master's instructions and attend to them with the ear of your heart." Finally, a monastic history will be the story of a search to use the monastic means to holiness. The story of the attainment of holiness only God can write. Human historians write of the means to holiness, of a place, and of a listening.

1882–1892

ardinal John Henry Newman called the early Middle Ages the "Benedictine centuries." By reason of its own intrinsic merits and the support of the Carolingian rulers, the *Rule of Benedict* enjoyed almost a monopoly in religious communities in Western Europe. This near monopoly lasted until the rise of new religious orders in the twelfth and thirteenth centuries. By that time the monastery of Engelberg in central Switzerland was flourishing. Founded in 1120, the abbey was already a center of learning and religious life under Blessed Abbot Frowin (deceased 1178).

For seven centuries more the abbey of Engelberg has endured, sometimes prospering, sometimes reduced to only a remnant. Around it grew up a town with the same name. To the religious needs of the townspeople, the monks ministered; the abbey church of Engelberg still serves as the parish church. Today the monastery operates a flourishing high school for local students and for boarders from elsewhere. But one hundred years ago, the continued existence of the abbey seemed in doubt.

Throughout the nineteenth century a number of Swiss religious communities had been suppressed, and in 1870 it was not certain that Engelberg, even though it was located in an overwhelmingly Catholic area, would be spared. As early as 1854, the Swiss abbey of Einsiedeln had founded the monastery of St. Meinrad in Indiana, and it seemed to the monks of Engelberg that they, too, should establish a place of possible refuge in a free land.

There were other incentives to draw the monks of Engelberg to America. Abbot Boniface Wimmer of St. Vincent Abbey in Pennsylvania had been urging European monasteries to help minister to the religious needs of German-speaking Catholics in America. Missionary work among the Indians also beckoned the Swiss monks.

In 1873 Abbot Anselm Villiger (deceased 1901) of Engelberg appointed Fathers Frowin Conrad and Adelhelm Odermatt to go to America. They traveled to St. Meinrad, then to the hamlet of Conception, in the diocese of St. Joseph, Missouri. A monastery building was already being built for them on the gently rolling land, and soon recruits for the monastery arrived from Switzerland. Already by April 15, 1881, the monastery was firmly enough established to become an abbey and, to form with St. Meinrad Abbey, the Swiss-American federation.

At the time the foundation at Conception became an abbey, the Swiss monks had to decide whether to transfer their vow of stability to the newly independent community or return to Engelberg. Father Adelhelm did not like these alternatives. He wishes to remain in America, where priests were needed badly, but he did not wish to join the new American abbey. In his view, Conception seemed to have departed too much from the venerable Swiss tradition in favor of monasticism championed by recently founded communities like Beuron in Germany.

Faced with this dilemma, Father Adelhelm thought of a third alternative. He urged Abbot Anselm to make a second Engelberg foundation in America, one that would be a much closer replica of Engelberg, and hence a more suitable place of refuge if Engelberg should be suppressed by the Swiss government.

Father Adelhelm set out with another Engelberg monk, Father Nicholas Frei, in search of a place to establish the new monastery. They traveled widely in the West, to Colorado and to California, eagerly examining possible sites. Eventually they came to Oregon; they had heard that the Rogue River Valley was a paradise, and Father Adelhelm wanted to see it. He went to Jacksonville, whose inhabitants urged the Benedictines to settle there.

Archbishop Charles John Seghers (archbishop 1880–1884) was very much interested in establishing the Benedictines in the archdiocese of Oregon City. He had been corresponding with Abbot Alexius Edelbrock of St. John's Abbey, Minnesota, a foundation of St. Vincent Abbey. In December, 1881, Abbot Alexius came to Oregon to look over the possibilities. He was not impressed: the climate was damp and dismal, the Catholic population meager, the number of clergy sufficient.

Meanwhile, in August, 1881, Archbishop Seghers had gone to the little town of Fillmore to bless a new church built there by the citizens, who were tired of going seven miles to Gervais for Mass. The guiding spirit of the Fillmore group of German Catholic families was Mathias Butsch. On August 21, 1881, Archbishop Seghers was in Fillmore to bless their new church. He took the opportunity to journey to the top of the nearby butte. There are several accounts of how he got there, but it seems certain that as he looked out over the valley from the top of the butte, he was struck with what a suitable spot the hilltop was for a religious institute or seminary. Perhaps he was thinking of the Swiss Benedictines who were looking for a monastic site.

When Fathers Adelhelm and Nicholas left Jacksonville, they visited the Archbishop, who asked them to take care of the church in Fillmore over a weekend. While the two Swiss monks were in Fillmore, Mr. Butsch took them to the top of the hill. Father Adelhelm was convinced: this place with its beautiful view, fertile land, and devout people was the site for a new Engelberg. During the winter, Father Adelhelm cared for the Catholic communities of Gervais, Sublimity and Fillmore, while Father Nicholas went to San Francisco to learn English and to investigate possible locations for a monastery in California.

In the spring of 1882, Father Adelhelm set out for Switzerland to obtain permission for the foundation in Oregon from his confreres at Engelberg, sisters to teach in Gervais and two Indian schools in Oregon, and recruits for his new foundation. He reached Engelberg on June 17 and obtained the permission and recruits. On the way back across America he recruited Mother Bernardine Wachter, O.S.B., whom he had known in Missouri, and several other Benedictine sisters who had come to America from the convents of Maria Rickenbach and St. Andrew (Sarnen) near Engelberg. On October 28 he arrived back in Portland with twenty-seven companions including, besides the sisters, three priests, one lay brother, and some student candidates.

The monks moved into the rectory at Gervais, where they stayed until the summer of 1884. On November 13, 1882, they began praying the divine office, a practice which has been maintained ever since. Father Adelhelm immediately set about acquiring title to the hill near Fillmore, called "Lone Butte" or "Graves Butte". To obtain ownership of this butte and some farm land, Prior Adelhelm had to borrow money and enter the land market. From 1882 to 1888 he purchased, at about $25.00 an acre, parcels of land amounting to over 1800 acres.

During these same years the foundation made rapid progress. The name of the town Fillmore was changed to Mount Angel. Plans were set in motion to build a monastery with a church which would serve both town and monks. Because it would be too expensive to build on the top of the hill, the monastery and church were constructed on the first rise of the hill, near where the abbey farm shops are today. The summer of 1884, the monks came to their new home. They started to farm, and priests from the priory served the Catholics in Gervais, Mount Angel, and Sublimity.

In 1883, the monastery had received recognition by the State of Oregon as a charitable corporation; Father Adelhelm, Father Barnabas Held, and Father Anselm Wachter (deceased 1907) were the corporation officers. The articles of incorporation mentioned educational work, and state authorities urged the monks to undertake educational work in the local area. In 1887 the monks issued a prospectus for Mount Angel College, which would offer classical and commercial courses to boarding and day students (at a five-month fee of $90.00 and $50.00 respectively).

The school was opened with about fifty students, in a two-story college building measuring thirty by thirty-five feet. The next year 130 students showed up, and the chapter voted to build a new college building. Permission was secured from Engelberg; Abbot Anselm hoped the school would help the new foundation pay off some of its debts. Before school was over that year, the students were occupying their new, 150 by 50 feet, four-story building. Across the road from the abbey building there were a library and a guest house.

From the beginning the monastic community at Mount Angel had close ties with the archdiocese of Oregon City (now Portland), the second oldest one in the United States. Archbishop Blanchet (1846–1880) was the first bishop. He was living in retirement when the monks arrived in 1882, but he received the founding band and laid his hands in blessing on the young man who as Father Maurus Snyder was the last of the founders to die (in 1958). Archbishop Seghers (1880–1884) returned to Canada in 1884 and was murdered several years later. He was succeeded by Archbishop William H. Gross, C.Ss.R. (1885–1898). The Mount Angel school catalogue for 1889–1890 announced that in accord with the latter's wishes minor and major seminary divisions were to be opened that year.

During the next few years the priory's schools prospered. With an enrollment of about 150 students, they required most of the personnel of the priory. To help free the monks for work in the school, the parishes of Gervais and Sublimity were returned to the care of diocesan pastors in 1888 and 1889, although in 1893 the parish of Sacred Heart in Portland was entrusted to the pastoral care of the monks.

The steady growth of the priory suffered a grave setback on May 3, 1892, when the priory roof caught fire. The building was quickly engulfed in flames. Everyone took or threw out whatever he could. Meanwhile, monks, students and lay people used bucket brigades and hoses to try to save the college building. They were successful, but the priory, chapel, seminary wing, and shops were smoking ruins. Only the college building and two other small buildings were still standing. The monks moved into these three buildings and began to try to rebuild their devastated priory.

Of the buildings of this era only one remains, a small, charming chapel now in the abbey cemetery. Right across from it lies the tombstone of Father Adelhelm, whose persistence, vision and hard work led to the foundation at Mount Angel and were now to make possible its continuance.

1882–1892

This painting shows Engelberg Abbey, in central Switzerland, and the surrounding valley around 1880, when the monks and sisters left Switzerland to found their respective communities in Oregon. The monks founded Mount Angel Abbey (now in Saint Benedict, Oregon) and the sisters who came from two different Swiss communities founded Queen of Angels Monastery (in Mt. Angel, Oregon) and the Monastery of St. Gertrude (in Cottonwood, Idaho).

Abbot Anselm Villiger, 52nd Abbot of Engelberg, who founded the Mount Angel Abbey community.

Fathers Frowin Conrad (left) and Adelhelm Odermatt (right), the two men sent to found Conception Abbey in Missouri in 1873.

1882–1892

Conception Abbey as it appeared on a postcard of the early 1900s.

Father Nicholas Frei, a monk of Engelberg Abbey, was the companion of Father Adelhelm. Together they sought a site for a new monastery on the West Coast. However, Nicholas never became a member of the community in Oregon.

Archbishop Francis Norbert Blanchet, the first Archbishop of Oregon City, which became the Archdiocese of Portland in Oregon. He was living in retirement at St. Vincent Hospital in Portland in 1882 when he received the founding band of monks.

1882–1892

Archbishop Charles Seghers, the second Archbishop of Oregon City (later Portland). He invited the founders to establish a monastery in Oregon.

Mr. Matthias Butsch, a leading citizen of the local German Catholic settlers in what was "Fillmore," later renamed Mt. Angel. In 1881 he and other devoted citizens encouraged the monks to found a monastery near the town, for a Catholic presence and to develop schools to teach their children.

The postcard sent by Archbishop Seghers to Mr. Mathias Butsch to inform him of the arrival of the Benedictines.

1882–1892

This drawing of a photo was retouched with images, here of flames, using a technique of the early 1900s. This is the most detailed image available of the church in Gervais, Oregon, where the monks began to pray the Divine Office, in late 1882. The church was built in 1875 and burned in 1894.

The pilgrimage chapel on top of the hill, which was used beginning in 1889. After the 1892 fire that burned the monastery complex at the base of the hill, the chapel was significantly increased in size and became the church for the monks when they moved to the top of the hill in 1903. This chapel was destroyed in the 1926 fire.

1882–1892

From left to right: St. Benedict's Priory, Chapel, Seminary, and College. From 1884–1892 this chapel served both the monks and the local parish. This complex burned in 1892.

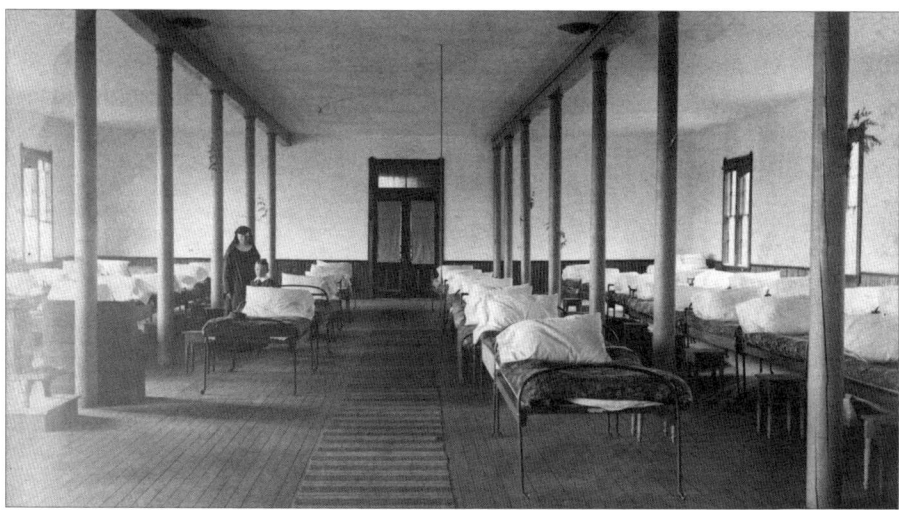

The interior of a dormitory in the college wing. Sister Ignatia, OSB, is standing beside a student. The Benedictine sisters cared for the students and dormitories.

1882–1892

An idealized drawing by Br. Anselm Weissenborn which was made a few days before the fire of May 3, 1892. Only the college, post office, and library remained. The central buildings burned. The wing of the priory labeled "New Church Contemplated" was never built.

The first faculty (1887–1888) of Mt. Angel College, which was a high school begun by the monks. The picture was taken in Gervais, where the community began. *Front row (left to right):* Fr. Leo Huebscher, Fr. Barnabas Held, Fr. Anselm Wachter, Fr. Dominic Waedenschwyler. *Back row (left to right):* Br. Theodulus Wuersch, Fr. Peter Beutgen (a diocesan priest), Fr. Maurus Snyder, Fr. Placidus Fuerst, Fr. William Kramer.

1882–1892

Interior of a classroom in Mt. Angel College (a high school) which was begun by the monks in 1887.

Most Reverend William Hickley Gross, CSsR, the third Archbishop of Oregon City and a member of the Redemptorist order. He asked the Benedictines to open the seminary in 1889.

1882–1892

The first seminary faculty and student body for 1889–90.

The monastic community in May of 1891 in front of a large tree near the college building at the foot of the hill.

1882–1892

Sacred Heart Parish in Southeast Portland was entrusted to the monks in 1893.

Saint Agatha's parish in Portland branched off from Sacred Heart in December of 1911. This church, pictured in this postcard, was built in 1921. Fr. John Cumminsky is the pastor pictured.

1892–1910

After this first disastrous fire, the priory had a debt of about $200,000. Not only were there no funds for rebuilding, there was even danger that the struggling community would lose its land. With Archbishop Gross' warm approval, Prior Adelhelm appealed for help in Oregon. He decided, then, to travel to the cities of the East to ask for funds. Prior Adelhelm and the monks underwent great physical hardships at this time; more agonizing still were the worry and fear for the foundation's survival which they shared with the abbot and monks of Engelberg.

Prior Adelhelm's money-raising efforts were successful enough to give the community hope. Abbot Anselm of Engelberg wrote: "Father Adelhelm, who had been so zealous in contracting debts, proved himself to be equally zealous in collecting the money to pay for them." However, Father Adelhelm's prolonged absences left the community without a leader. Moreover, he was not a careful financial manager. In order to provide more leadership and financial management in the community, the Abbot of Engelberg sent out a new prior, Father Benedict Gottwald, one of the ablest monks at Engelberg. It was his task to guide the young community through some of its darkest days. He grappled with the heavy debt, the poor housing conditions, the disturbed monastic observance. He was a stern man, but also a sensitive one. After five years as prior, he returned to Switzerland, exhausted from his labors.

Before any rebuilding was begun, two decisive steps were taken. The town of Mount Angel had been using the priory chapel. Now that this had burned down, it was decided to build a new parish church closer to the center of town. This church was replaced in 1912 by the imposing brick church which the parish uses to this day.

Now that the Parish had its own church, the monastic community had more freedom about where they would rebuild their monastery and church. Some monks wished to move to the top of the hill, while others argued vigorously for a more economical reconstruction on the original site. Ultimately, the Abbot of Engelberg, Father Adelhelm and the community decided to build this time on the top of the hill. Already by March 1883, a small chapel had been built at the site of the future cemetery. In 1889 a new larger chapel was built on the top of the hill, which was enlarged again and again, even while it served as the monastery's church until 1926. Slowly and laboriously Brother Magnus Blarer (deceased 1905) and some helpers began to quarry stone for the new monastery. The stones they carved out of the hill are still used in the wall surrounding the monastic garden.

In 1898, back in Switzerland, Abbot Anselm, now old and feeble, decided to appoint Abbot Frowin Conrad of Conception Abbey as his delegate of visitation for Mount Angel. Abbot Anselm died in 1901, but his successor, Abbot Leodegar Scherer, confirmed the delegation of Abbot Frowin. He instructed Abbot Frowin to conduct a thorough evaluation and study of Mount Angel's discipline and finances, and then to hold the election of a new prior.

Father Thomas Meienhofer, who had the respect of both Abbot Leodegar and Abbot Frowin, was elected prior on July 11, 1901. He immediately set to work to incorporate Mount Angel into the Swiss-American Federation, to finish the new monastery on the hill, and to have the priory made an independent monastery. For twenty years some of the Mount Angel community had been resisting affiliation with the Swiss-American Federation, because they felt it was too much influenced by customs and ideas alien to the Swiss Benedictine tradition. In 1902 the juridical issue was settled, as Mount Angel entered the Swiss-American Federation, which by that time included five independent American monasteries. The feelings and differences symbolized by "Beuronese" and "Swiss" would persist for decades.

Within two years the community was able to complete the monastery on the hilltop. A college wing was added, even though Father Adelhelm's plan had been to leave the college at the foot of the hill and reserve the hilltop for abbey, seminary and shrine to St. Joseph. From Christmas Eve, 1903, the community of Mount Angel lived in its place on the hill.

For some years the status of Mount Angel as a priory dependent on Engelberg had been a source of difficulty. Ultimate authority lay with the abbot and chapter of Engelberg, seven thousand miles away. This caused delays in communication, and it meant too that members of the Mount Angel community could appeal to Engelberg, thereby lessening the local prior's authority. Prior Thomas felt that Mount Angel should become independent so that the local prior would have full authority. With some reluctance Abbot Leodegar consented. Abbot Frowin came out from Conception and supervised an election for the man to be presented to Rome for appointment as abbot of the newly independent community. Father Thomas was elected on the ninth ballot. Abbot Leodegar was pleased with the choice; he sent from Engelberg an abbatial cross for the new abbot, one still used by the abbots of Mount Angel.

On March 24, 1904, Pope Pius X made Mount Angel an abbey and appointed Father Thomas the first abbot. He was blessed on June 29, 1904, in the presence of his community, many bishops, and the Governor of Oregon.

Independence and entry into the Swiss-American Federation did not mean severing all bonds with Engelberg. Many monks of Mount Angel have since enjoyed the hospitality of the monastery at Engelberg. Moreover, the new community still owed a substantial amount of money to the community at Engelberg. In 1904 these debts were consolidated on terms very favorable to the new abbey. On November 6, 1981, the monastic chapter of Engelberg voted unanimously to cancel the still considerable remainder of these debts as a token of the fellowship between the two communities.

During these early years the community began another new enterprise. Both St. Meinrad and Conception had been engaged in missionary work among the Indians, and now Mount Angel was asked to provide missionaries among the Indians on the west coast of Vancouver Island, an isolated primitive area with over one hundred inches of rainfall a year. In 1899, the community accepted this new challenge, and the next year the first two missionaries were sent north. Sisters from Queen of Angels Convent joined the enterprise. The missions included a school at Kakawis and coastal mission stations accessible only by canoe. Of all the missionaries sent to Vancouver Island, Father Charles Moser labored there the longest. In 1926 he published a volume of reminiscences of missionary work on the west coast of Vancouver Island; the narratives of the book reveal the dedication and difficulties of those who brought Christianity to the Indian tribes there.

During the early part of this century, the community grew steadily in numbers and apostolates. The enrollment in the abbey schools ranged between 90 and 150. Gradually other schools took over education of the youngest students, and the abbey concentrated its educational efforts in high school, college and theology programs. The student body included both day students and boarders; the latter included lay students and seminarians, who resided in separate wings, but had classes together.

Although the work of the school accelerated the transition from German to English, the abbey did edit and publish a German-language weekly newspaper, the *St. Joseph Blatt*. The abbey had taken the paper over in the early 1890s; by 1909 this enterprise required the building of a new press building, to the north of the abbey. (This building still houses our press services; it is to the north of the present gymnasium.) The paper had a colorful and useful career. At times circulation exceeded 50,000. The emphasis of the paper was the preservation of German-speaking immigrants' Catholic heritage, but it had many subscribers in Europe. Brother Coelestine Mueller (deceased 1929) was a noteworthy editor; he wrote great amounts of copy in a trenchant German style. During the First World War the *Blatt* was suppressed by the government as too pro-German, but the paper was restarted after the war. The abbey continued to publish the *Blatt* regularly until 1966, when it was finally sold. The abbey published a number of other German and English language periodicals. The most long-lived of these was the *St. Joseph Magazine,* a Catholic monthly which maintained high professional standards under the editorship of Father Albert Bauman (professed as a monk 1936). In recent years the abbey has issued no regular publications, except a newsletter, *The Mount Angel Letter*.

In spite of the progress achieved under Abbot Thomas Meienhofer, there were tensions which discouraged and saddened the Abbot. Eventually these put so much strain on him and his health that on May 25, 1910, he resigned his position. When he then left the religious life and moved to the East Coast, the community was crushed. The newspapers gave the Abbot's leaving embarrassing publicity.

1892–1910

Father Benedict Gottwald, OSB, was sent by Abbot Anselm Villiger from the mother house in Switzerland, 1894–1899. He was given a challenging assignment: save the priory in Oregon, which he did. He led the community after the devastating fire of 1892.

Church buildings in Mt. Angel during the late 1910s: *Top, Left:* The third church in Mt. Angel, with the steeple removed; *Top, Right:* The parish school; *Bottom, Center:* The "parsonage" or rectory of the parish.

The town of Mt. Angel in 1908, as seen looking east from the site of the old Mt. Angel Hotel. At the top center of the photo is the third church in Mt. Angel; it was replaced by the current church in 1912. At the upper right, on the flank of he Abbey hill stands the old college building, which remained after the 1892 fire burned most of the priory buildings.

The town of Mt. Angel in 1908, as seen looking west from the site of the old priory.

1892–1910

The dedication of the fourth and current church of Mt. Angel in 1912.

The break between ballotings at the election of Fr. Thomas Meienhofer as Prior around noon on July 11, 1901.

1892–1910

Abbot Thomas Meienhofer, OSB, at the time of his election in 1904.

Dignitaries and community assembled for Abbot Thomas' blessing on June 29, 1904. Governor Chamberlain was present and is seated with legs crossed and cigar in hand in the front center.

The arch at the foot of the hill, which marked the boundary for the students.

1892–1910

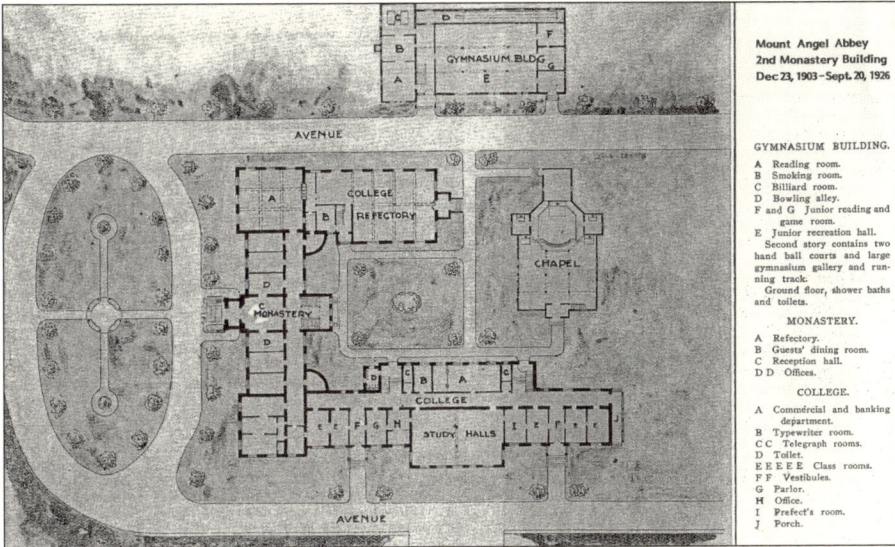

A 1902 diagram of the principal buildings on the Abbey Hilltop, along with the principal rooms. This building complex included the second monastery. The angel garden is at the left. The buildings and uses of principal rooms are noted at the right.

A photograph of the second monastery. It was the central portion of the building complex constructed on top of the hill in the late 1890s and early 1900s. The monks occupied the building from Christmas Eve, December 24, 1903 until September 20, 1926, when the complex burned. This image was made about 1925, when the building was at the height of its development. It was slightly retouched with paint to give the building a more finished look. The crosses at the top of the building were painted on, as were the conical trees at the bottom of the picture.

1892–1910

The dream that the monks had. The church was to be in the center, facing south. The part to the left of the church was completed in 1903. The surface of the building was not white, as the image shows, but nearly black, made with basalt stone blocks. The church and building to the right were envisioned, but were never constructed.

The angel garden in front of the second monastery. The angel statue is still at the Abbey, between the church and the retreat house. The press building and post office are visible at the right of the photo.

1892–1910

The pilgrimage chapel on top of the hill was used beginning in 1889. After the 1892 fire the chapel was added to significantly (as is shown in this photograph). The previous pilgrimage chapel then became the church for the monks when they moved to the top of the hill in 1903. This chapel and all the buildings shown in this picture were ultimately destroyed in the 1926 fire.

The town of Mt. Angel, looking east to the Abbey butte, about 1910. The second monastery building complex, of the monks, is in the center of the photo. The monastery of the Benedictine sisters is at the right.

The monastery of the Benedictine sisters, in the late 1800s. At that time the sisters lived in the part of the building on the left while the girls who were students in their boarding school lived in the part of the building on the right.

1892–1910

Fr. Charles Moser, missionary to the Indians on Vancouver Island.

A group picture taken at Christie School, for Indian children, on the west coast of Vancouver Island, British Columbia. At the right is Fr. Charles Moser. At the top row were four Benedictine sisters who served along with the monks.

The Christie School, for Indian children, on the west coast of Vancouver Island, British Columbia.

1892–1910

Another perspective of the Christie School, Vancouver Island, British Columbia.

Br. Coelestine Mueller, editor of the St. Joseph's Blatt, in 1895.

1892–1910

Two monks and an employee preparing text to be printed at the Benedictine Press.

At the Benedictine Press, mailing the weekly *St. Joseph Blatt,* the weekly German-language newspaper that monks and hired staff prepared, printed and mailed to subscribers across the U.S.

The Benedictine Press building, and U.S. Post Office of St. Benedict, Oregon. German and English-language newspapers mailed from here helped to bring people of German heritage to the town of Mt. Angel, as well as to its two Benedictine communities.

1892–1910

Fr. Placidus Fuerst (later, Abbot) and his sister, Sister Beatrice of the Queen of Angels Priory.

A scene from the abbey land: a tractor operating a processing machine. From the 1890s until the Abbey leased out its lands in 1976 the monks and their workers were agricultural innovators in the Willamette Valley. Note the second monastery complex on the abbey hill, behind the machinery.

1910–1930

n August 30, 1910, the community gathered to elect a new abbot. They chose Father Placidus Fuerst who had been born in Germany in 1868. One of Father Adelhelm's earliest recruits, Abbot Placidus was proud of the community's Swiss heritage. Like his contemporary, Father Dominic Waedenschwyler (deceased 1932), Abbot Placidus was an accomplished musician and composer. At the time of his election, Abbot Placidus was pastor of Mount Angel parish. He accepted his new task out of a sense of duty to church and community, but he never was happy with the position.

He guided the abbey through the difficult years of World War I. In the school a large flag was decorated with stars indicating how many alumni of the school, staffed largely by professors of German-speaking backgrounds, were in the armed services of the United States. One member of the community, Father Ildephonse Calmus, enlisted as a chaplain. In later years, others followed him into the armed forces as chaplains: Father Lawrence Eskay (deceased 1974), Father Bertrand McLaughlin (deceased 1990) and Father Leo Rimmele (professed 1950).

By the time of Father Placidus' election, Father Adelhelm was over sixty-five years old. In 1916 Father Adelhelm celebrated his golden jubilee of profession and was made titular abbot. The venerated patriarch greatly appreciated this honor, and during his remaining years he pontificated throughout the diocese with plenty of incense and ornate ceremony. He died in 1920, after suffering a stroke at St. Joseph parish in Portland, where he was assisting.

In 1917 Father Basil Schieber (deceased 1919) became pastor of the Catholics in Tillamook county. This began over sixty years of ministry by priests of the abbey to the Tillamook area. Among those who served there the longest were Father Hildebrand Melchior (deceased 1977), who was responsible for building the churches in Cloverdale and Rockaway; Father Raphel Bleummel (deceased 1965); Father Vincent Koppert (deceased 1985); Father Francis Burger (deceased 1966); Father Matthew Butsch (deceased 2001); and Father Richard Galvin (deceased 2003). In 1980 a diocesan priest became pastor of Tillamook, but Father Edward Spear (deceased 1991) continued as pastor of Rockaway.

Unlike Father Adelhelm, Father Placidus did not relish being an abbot. The stability and morale of the abbey seemed to be solid enough that he could resign the office on July 5, 1921. He had built few buildings (the post office and a barn), but he had served the community well by his exemplary life and his devotion. Once relieved of the abbatial burden, he spent some time resting at the Indian missions; then he became pastor of St. Joseph's German parish in Portland. Refusing the title and insignia of abbot, he served as a wise and kind pastor. He died in 1940.

On October 26, 1921, the community elected their new abbot, Father Bernard Murphy. Abbot Bernard had been born in Portland, December 10, 1874. The community was now increasingly made up of native-born Americans. Henceforth, no recruits would be accepted from Europe unless they had spent at least a year in the seminary to learn the English language and American customs. Further, the German-language divine office of the lay brothers no longer served the needs of the few American-born brothers, so an English office was set up for them.

The first part of the decade was a time of steady growth. The school progressed well. The junior college division was recognized by the University of Oregon. Abbot Bernard started saving funds to replace the ramshackle chapel. No new building projects were undertaken, although Father Victor Rassier (deceased 1964) did have the students help build a cement wall along the south side of the hilltop, to prevent players and balls from tumbling over the edge of the playing field. The picturesque wall remains one of the few surviving physical tokens of that area.

During the night of September 20, 1926, twenty-three years after it was first occupied, the entire abbey and school complex burned to the ground. The fire began in a wooden garage between the carpenter shop and the gymnasium. The night was rainy and windy when the night watchman sounded the alarm at 11:30. The fire soon caused a power outage, so that there was no way to pump water to the hilltop. Abbot Bernard retired to the little chapel in the cemetery to pray. The next morning nothing was left standing except the press and the adjoining post office building, and these were endangered by sparks from the soldering ruins. A pump truck from Salem kept their roofs wetted down, and they were saved. They became the means by which the now homeless monks would appeal for help to Catholics throughout the country.

The community went to the parish church in Mount Angel to pray the morning office; they would hold community prayers there for the next eighteen months. The monks took up residence in some rented houses and the old parish school. The seminary was moved to two large private houses, but no non-seminary boarders were accepted into the college after the fire. Monastic and school life were soon reconstituted on a makeshift basis, but there remained the massive task of rebuilding.

Abbot Bernard and his prior, Father Jerome Wespe (deceased 1954), had both lived through the difficult years that followed the fire of 1892. They were determined to rebuild the monastery as soon as possible. Expenses were curtailed as much as possible, and all expendable assets were sold, except for the farm land which was kept inviolate as a basis for the future. The community sent out appeals to the readers of the abbey's publications, and several of the monks, including Fathers Gabriel Morrisroe (deceased 1962), Michael Reilly (deceased 1985) and Alcuin Heibel (deceased 1985), traveled around the country to collect money.

After long discussions, it was decided to rebuild on the top of the hill, but the abbey was to be located on the back side of the hill to assure the community seclusion and quiet. The design of the building was influenced by the memory of the fires which had twice destroyed the community's home. The buildings would not form a tight medieval enclosed square, but would be far enough apart so that a fire in one would not doom the others. A large free-standing water tank would be erected, and the power lines would be arranged for maximum safety. The buildings would be of concrete, with brick facing.

Work began on the new abbey building late in the spring of 1927. Originally the plans called for a four-story building to be the home for a community of 100 monks. However, there were sufficient funds for only three stories. The church building fund, which Abbot Bernard had started before the fire, was sufficient to build the sanctuary for a new church, to which was added a temporary nave that could seat about one hundred people. Even this restricted rebuilding placed a heavy financial strain on the community, and two decades would be required to pay off the debts. The monks pledged themselves to celebrate the daily community Mass perpetually for the benefactors, who made the rebuilding possible.

Finally, on the Feast of St. Joseph, May 19, 1928, after the community celebrated Mass in the parish church in Mount Angel, a procession was formed and moved joyously up the hill to the new abbey which stood proudly amid a sea of mud and construction debris. On March 21, Archbishop Edward Howard (1926–1966) blessed the new chapel and extended his best wishes to the community.

The abbey schools also returned to the hilltop. The seminary was squeezed into the south end of the abbey building; day students were being taught in the basement. This overcrowded situation was not tolerated for long. In spite of the abbey's debts and the onslaught of the Depression, some generous benefactors were found. Construction was hurried along, and what is today Aquinas Hall was sufficiently completed for partial occupancy in September, 1930.

1910–1930

The community, gathered after the election of Abbot Placidus Fuerst, on August 30, 1910.

Abbot Placidus Fuerst at the time of his election and abbatial blessing.

The World War I service flag for the abbey and school.

1910–1930

Farmers' picnic at Hall's farm in July, 1915. Fr. Adelhelm Odermatt and Fr. Bonaventure Huesser are in the back of the buggy. Br. Peter Baier is the driver, and Fr. Hildebrand Melchior is beside him.

Titular Abbot Adhelhelm Odermatt, taken about 1916, when he was given the title of Abbot.

Madame Schumann-Heink assisted at the Sept. 29, 1916 golden jubilee celebration of Abbot Adelhelm Odermatt, O.S.B., founder of Mount Angel Abbey. Also shown is Bishop A.F. Schinner of Spokane.

1910–1930

The parish church in Tillamook of which the monks took charge in 1917.

The parish church in Tillamook, dedicated in 1970. The monks serving in this parish established two mission churches in Tillamook County and provided pastoral care in the area until 1981.

1910–1930

St. Joseph Church in Cloverdale, Oregon, on the coast. This church was built in 1921 and was staffed by monks of Mount Angel until 1981, when it was turned over to the Archdiocese of Portland. This church is a mission church of Sacred Heart Parish in Tillamook.

St. Mary's by the Sea, in Rockaway, Oregon. This church was built in 1927 and was staffed by monks of Mount Angel until 1981, when it was turned over to the Archdiocese of Portland. This church was a mission church of Sacred Heart Parish in Tillamook.

1910–1930

The group of men who attended the first lay reatreat held at the Abbey. The picture was taken in 1920 and was one of the last pictures taken of Fr. Abbot Adelhelm Odermatt, who is in the center of the first row. He died later that year.

Inside the chapel on top of the hill which served as a temporary church for the monks during the time of the second monastery. This was the first Mass of a newly-ordained priest.

1910–1930

The sports field in the spring of 1926. The location of the origin of the fire is visible: the garage with door open, across the road and to the right of the chapel.

The light in this photo is from the flames of the fire that began in the nearby garage on the evening of September 20, 1926. By the next morning all these buildings were in ashes.

1910–1930

A dream realized, 1903 – 1925

A disaster suffered, 1926

1910–1930

The ruins from the north side of the hill.

The inner court of the abbey in ruins.

Inside the remnants of the college wing. The wooden floors burned away, sending all remaining materials into the basement.

1910–1930

The buildings at the "Milk Ranch" property, during the early 1900s. The property is in the foothills of the Cascade mountains, about 15 miles east of the Abbey butte. The monks have owned over 2500 acres of forest there since the 1880s. It has been a source of income, initially for feeding milk cows, then since the 1920s for lumber.

Abbot Primate Fidelis von Stotzingen, the titular leader of the Order of Saint Benedict, had visited the monks before the September 20-21, 1926 fire. He returned soon to the Abbey from Cottonwood, Idaho, when he heard about the fire. The photo was taken at the entrance to the monastery of the Benedictine sisters, Queen of Angels, in Mt. Angel. Each monk is identified by a number: 1. Father Dominic, 2. Abbot Primate Fidelis, Abbot Bernard, 4. Father Victor, 5. Frater Paul ("Frater" means he was preparing to be ordained as a priest), 6. Father Cyril, 7. Frater Mark, 8. Father Bonaventure, 9. Father Leo, 10. Frater Anthony, 11. Father Sebastian, 12. Father Alphonse, 13. Frater Damian.

The Abbey clerics (monks studying for the priesthood) in the late 1920s.

1910–1930

Fr. Alcuin Heibel the day in the 1970s that he received an award from Pope Paul VI. The pope honored Fr. Alcuin for his work to collect money and purchase necessities of life from the U.S., then ship the thousands of boxes to Europe. He did this to help alleviate suffering caused by World War II.

Fr. Michael Reilly, who was well known, especially the 1950s–1970s, for his pastoral work in parishes across the State of Oregon.

Father Gabriel Morris, OSB, was well-known around the Pacific Northwest for the retreats and parish missions he presented.

1910–1930

Work progressing on the third monastery (the current one) on July 21, 1927. This view is looking toward the southwest. The area in the foreground is the monastery refectory (dining room).

Aerial view of Mount Angel Abbey and the city of Mt. Angel, taken about late 1928. Note that the current Abbey church is not completed; it was finally completed in 1952. The ruins of the second monastery (which burned in 1926) are removed; they were located between the monastery and the largest group of trees in this photo.

Mount Angel Hilltop
25 years ago
1. Seminary Site
2. College wing
3. Abbey
4. Chapel
5. Gymnasium
6. Garage (fire start)
7. Carpenter shop
8. Sister's house
9. Flower garden
10. Storage bldg.
11. Printing shop
12. Cemetery
13. Old vineyard
14. Backstop & ball diamond

Aerial view of Mount Angel Abbey taken about late 1928. This view has numbered items, which identify the locations of the ruins of the second monastery. The building at the upper left is the third monastery (the current one) which was still under construction.

1910–1930

The current monestary being built in early 1928.

Laying of the cornerstone on July 17, 1927. Left to right: Fr. Maurus Snyder; Abbot Bernard; Fr. Sebastian Terhaar, M.C.; Robert Barrett, the architect; his brother, Edward Barrett, the general contractor, is behind him. At the right, looking on, is the foreman of the works.

1910–1930

The abbey bells, which were secured by Peter Mayer, who had been a member of the community and contributed the cost of the second largest bell. The bells were cast by Stuckside & Brothers Foundry, St. Louis, Missouri and were blessed by Abbot Bernard on March 18, 1928. The size of the bells: The Holy Family (1478 pounds), The Little Flower & St. Rita (800 pounds), St. Benedict & St. Scholastica (460 pounds) and St. Michael (100 pounds).

The present monastery, during final construction phases in 1928.

1910–1930

Drawing of an imaginary aerial view (completed November, 1929) of the Abbey Hilltop, done by the same architectural firm which designed the current Abbey church. Note, the balanced arrangement of the buildings and the church bell towers.

Aquinas Hall soon after completion in 1930.

1930–1950

The strain of the fire and rebuilding had worn out Abbot Bernard. His poor eyesight worsened until he was totally blind. He decided that he should relinquish his office to a more robust man. On August 1, 1934, the community elected his successor, Father Thomas Meier, a forty-seven year old priest of Swiss ancestry, who had lived in Oregon almost all his life. Abbot Thomas had been novice master, cleric master and subprior; he had visited European monasteries and Conception abbey. A strong-willed man, he quickly set about formulating and implementing a wide range of projects.

He turned his attention to the living quarters of the ten Benedictine sisters who worked on the hilltop. Their quarters in the upstairs of the post office building were totally inadequate. Under the direction of Father Hilary Grantz (deceased 1982), a house was built for them near the abbey kitchen. This house was the center for the apostolate among that local Russian Old Believers, conducted by Brother Ambrose Moorman (professed 1956) until recently.

Next, Abbot Thomas joined together the German and English brothers in a single chapel and introduced an English version of the divine office for them. He also improved the brothers' spiritual formation by regular conferences, and their recreation by improved facilities.

Abbot Thomas was deeply committed to the then burgeoning liturgical movement. He insisted on the use of Gregorian chant, and sent Father Victor Rassier to study chant for a year at the French abbey of Solesmes. The sanctuary and choir area of the church were furnished as nicely as possible—with the carved lectern, the choir stalls begun by Brother Gabriel Loerch (deceased 1932), and the mosaic floor—all of which are still there today.

As a result of the fire, a number of young monks were sent to Europe to finish their studies. Among these were Father Luke Eberle (deceased 1995) and Father Martin Pollard (deceased 1997). Both men were long involved in the religious formation of the younger members of the abbey, and Father Martin was prior for twenty-five years. In 1931, the two young monks purchased the entire stock of a used bookstore in Aachen, Germany, which became the nucleus of the abbey library.

Under the impetus of Father Alcuin Heibel (deceased 1985), the abbey schools received full accreditation. The gymnasium-auditorium was built in 1936, and in 1946 the athletic field was completed on the south side of the hill.

War surplus wooden buildings were purchased to provide classrooms for the day high school and a gymnasium for the seminarians. In 1947 the community made the difficult and hotly debated decision to close the lay college part of the school and concentrate its efforts on the education of seminarians.

In 1935 Abbot Thomas announced he had received an invitation to establish on the mainland of British Columbia a monastery where the divine office would be celebrated and seminarians trained. In 1938 the Indian missions on Vancouver Island were turned over to the Oblates of Mary Immaculate. On the Feast of the Holy Cross, September 14, 1939, the founding band of Mount Angel monks set out for Canada to make their first foundation, Westminster.

The community at home pledged itself to pray a litany to St. Joseph every day, asking that the Saint intercede for the men and goods needed for the new foundation and the community at home. The community stills prays this litany after the evening meal. The new foundation became independent June 1, 1948; it was raised to an abbey on February 12, 1953.

Abbot Thomas was also concerned that monastic observances at Mount Angel conform to the norms of the Swiss-American Federation. His efforts to assure that this was so gave him the name and the tensions of a "reformer." He was successful in what he set out to do, and allowed no opposition to deter him. He enforced the strict observance of silence in the monastery. He set up a supply store which purchased commonly used items at cheap, bulk rates and distributed them to the monks as they had need.

Throughout his years in office, existing debts were paid off, and a fund to complete the church building was built up. Finally in 1950, there was sufficient capital to begin work. It was decided to build an underground church beneath the new nave; this crypt would be available for the needs of retreatants and seminarians. In the spring, work on the church and crypt began.

Meanwhile, Abbot Thomas' health was deteriorating. He suffered from high blood pressure and glaucoma. He lost one eye and at the recommendation of his doctors decided go give up the abbatial duties, which were putting such a strain upon him. He lived another eleven years in the monastery, mellowing with the years and esteemed for the wide-ranging accomplishments of his sixteen years as abbot.

1930–1950

The community on the election day of Abbot Thomas, August 1, 1934, on the south side of the abbey church.

Abbatial blessing of Abbot Thomas Meier at St. Mary's Church in Mt. Angel.

Fr. Victor Rassier, who was appointed choir master under Abbot Thomas.

1930–1950

Br. Gabriel Loersch, who was the abbey carpenter for over 30 years. He and Joe Foltz made the choir stalls which are in the abbey church. The small boy is a relative of Br. Gabriel.

This manuscript, which is kept in the rare book vault in the library, is representative of the books which the monks began to collect after the construction of the current monastery, in 1928. In 1933 several monks from the Abbey, who were then studying in Europe, acquired thousands of printed books from a book dealer named Kreutzer, who went bankrupt in Aachen, Germany. Those books helped to replace the thousands of library books which had been destroyed in the 1926 fire.

Ordination of Father Method Korn, May 6, 1937.

1930–1950

Br. Fidelis Schoenenberger feeding chickens at "porcopolis" (literally "Pig City") on the north side of the hill where the pigs and chickens were raised.

At the lower part of the picture are the high school buildings which arrived at the Abbey butte in 1946. During World War II the buildings had been constructed at Camp Adair, near Corvallis, they were taken apart, transported, and rebuilt at the new site.

The blessing of the foundation cross and the founding monks, on the occasion of their departure. On the Feast of the Holy Cross, September 14, 1939, the monks were sent to establish the first foundation of Mount Angel Abbey. It became Westminster Abbey, in Mission, British Columbia.

1930–1950

The third, and current, location of Westminster Abbey in Mission, British Columbia. The site overlooks the Fraser River.

Digging the crypt, before completing the Abbey church, in 1950.

Construction of the abbey church in 1951.

1930–1950

Some of the half-mile of shelves in the monastery attic, used to store books, before the construction of the Alvar Aalto Library.

Otto von Hapsburg on his visit to the abbey, with Abbot Thomas, on Oct. 13, 1949, when Archduke Otto was traveling throughout the United States.

1950–1974

On August 16, 1950, Father Damian Jentges, the pastor of Mount Angel parish and professor of moral theology in the seminary, was elected abbot on the first ballot. Raised in Idaho, he had attended Mount Angel Seminary for eight years before joining the abbey in 1926. In 1927 he went to the University of Salzburg, where he graduated with a doctorate in theology. He began teaching in the seminary in 1931 and was rector from 1939 to 1945. Right to the time of his death, Abbot Damian was an extremely conscientious worker. Although strict with himself, he disliked confrontations and preferred to give other people the benefit of the doubt.

His first task was to take in hand the construction of the church begun under Abbot Thomas. He decided to table the plan to build a bell tower, but to go ahead quickly with the crypt. On March 21, 1952, Abbot Thomas presided at a festive liturgy in the new church, which Archbishop Howard blessed. For the first time, the community at Mount Angel had an adequate church.

After the Second World War, the seminary was thriving under the leadership of Father Justin Reilly (deceased 1960), Father Bernard Sander (deceased 2008), and Father Ambrose Zenner (deceased 1976). The student body soon outgrew Aquinas Hall. In 1954 a new building, Anselm Hall, was constructed to house the minor seminary. To build the new complex, the community had to borrow money again, but it was now possible to retire the debt more quickly.

This made it possible for Abbot Damian to turn his attention to an apostolate dear to him: retreats. As early as 1920 retreats were held at the abbey during the summer months, when the seminary buildings were vacant. Now Abbot Damian wanted to have a year-round facility. While not all the community shared his enthusiasm for retreat work, most recognized the need for improved guest facilities. So construction on a guest-retreat house was begun in 1959. The building completed the next year could accommodate forty overnight guests.

While the hospitality apostolate of the community expanded, educational activities were somewhat curtailed by the removal of the day school from the hilltop. In August, 1959, a new high school was opened in the town of Mount Angel, later became coeducational, superseding the separate schools for boys and girls that the abbey and convent had operated since shortly after the first monks and nuns had come from Switzerland. The new school went through several subsequent metamorphoses, until today it is John F. Kennedy Public High School.

The buoyancy and hopes of the 1950s carried over into the early 1960s as vocations increased, finances remained sound, and the Vatican Council II opened new windows and vistas. It was easy to be optimistic and hopeful about the future. When strong pleas came from the Bishop of Cuernavaca, Mexico, and strong pressure came from the Vatican in support of Latin American missions, the Abbot was forced to consider the possibility of a Latin American foundation. At the same time, the Bishop of Boise, Idaho, urged that Mount Angel make a foundation in his diocese. Abbot Damian presented both invitations to the chapter. They chose to accept both invitations. Both foundations were originally conceived in connection with seminary work, though this never materialized in Idaho and was short-lived in Mexico.

In 1965 Father Ambrose Zenner was sent to Mexico with Brother Boniface Arechederra (professed 1956) to begin the priory there, and Father Patrick Meagher (deceased 1998) was put in charge of the Idaho venture. The foundation in Idaho built and staffed a Newman center in Twin Falls, while that in Mexico tried various apostolates and means of self-support.

Soon the shining hopes which had inspired these foundations began to tarnish. Vatican II brought new possibilities, but also new problems. Student unrest reached the seminaries; theologians challenged many cherished assumptions; some fundamental monastic values seemed to be questioned. Abbot Damian, a man of great moderation and love for tradition, was deeply pained by these new developments. His concerns were shared by the new Archbishop of Portland, Robert J. Dwyer (1966–1974), who became a good friend of the monastery and seminary.

In the area of liturgy the forces of change were irresistible. The venerable Latin liturgy, and its accompanying chants, were replaced by English. The order of the psalms in the divine office, largely unchanged since St. Benedict's day, was redone. The stately liturgical books were replaced by leaflets and mimeographed breviaries. At first, Mount Angel was able to take advantage of the new situation, as three members of the community began composing new liturgical music. Gradually, though, the situation changed, and the community found itself with no composers and a dearth of organists. On the other hand, a version of Vespers was produced which met with widespread acceptance in the community. The community to this day still has many liturgical possibilities to explore, including a remodeling of the church.

The introduction of English in the liturgy made it possible to combine the brothers' prayer with that of the abbey's priests and priesthood candidates. This change was accompanied by a revision in church law which made it possible for brothers to be fully integrated in the chapter and apostolates of the community. The distinction between lay brothers and solemnly professed choir monks was abolished; all could henceforth share the same rights and responsibilities. This integration has had many advantages, but it has also made it necessary to reconsider entrance requirements and educational and formational programs for new members in the community.

For some monks the upheavals of the decade after Vatican II were too much to bear. A number of priests and brothers left the community. Although candidates still continued to present themselves, few persevered. Today the community has only nine members who professed their first vows between 1961 and 1972.

Although his last years in office were troubled by the turmoil of the era, Abbot Damian was able to rejoice in the completion of some significant building projects. In 1968 a covered swimming pool, financed by the seminary parents' club, was completed under the skilled supervision of Fred Baumgartner, the father of Father Andrew (professed 1955). The pool was well utilized by monks, seminarians, and people from the surrounding area. In 1969, a large shop and warehouse complex was built on the east end of the hill behind the monastery.

By far the greatest monument to Abbot Damian's later years is the library. Already in 1963 he indicated that the monastery and seminary had to have an adequate library. Father Barnabas Reasoner (professed 1944), then the head librarian, contacted several world renowned architects and was able to secure the agreement of Alvar Aalto to design the new structure. In 1964 the community voted to undertake the project. Photographs and surveyors' reports were sent to Helsinki, Finland where Mr. Aalto worked to design a serviceable and beautiful building which would fit into the site and harmonize with existing buildings.

Meanwhile, anonymous donors, since identified as Howard and Jean Vollum, offered over $1,000,000 to pay for the project. Mr. and Mrs. Aalto visited the abbey and looked over the site. Groundbreaking took place in August, 1968, and the building solemnly dedicated on May 29–31, 1970. Prior to that over 50,000 books had been carried to the new library from various locations around the hilltop. For the first time in the twentieth century, the community of Mount Angel Abbey had a separate library building, and the hilltop was now graced by an architectural masterpiece.

Like Abbot Placidus, Abbot Damian had a great love of music. Perhaps recalling the music festivals he had known during his student days in Salzburg, Austria, he began a Bach Festival in 1972, which has continued since under the direction of Mrs. Michel MacKay.

By this time the strains of over twenty years in office were deeply etched in Abbot Damian's face. He was unable to keep up with his correspondence or to interact easily with many members of his community. Although he was weighed down by the burdens of his task, he continued without complaint in the office he believed God had given him. In August, 1974, he was found to have advanced cancer of the spine. He saw in this the signal that it was time to resign. He wrote out a resignation which was to take effect September 9, 1974, so that he might receive the vows of some of the young monks on the traditional day of September 8. He died, however, on September 1, still in office after twenty-four years.

During this quarter century the buildings of the abbey were doubled and paid for, two foundations begun, and the uncertainty of the 1960s and the early 1970s weathered. At the time of Abbot Damian's death, Father Anselm Galvin was prior and Father Bonaventure Zerr, subprior. These two men were to be Abbot Damian's successors in the abbatial office.

Blessing of the recently completed abbey church, March 21, 1952.

1950–1974

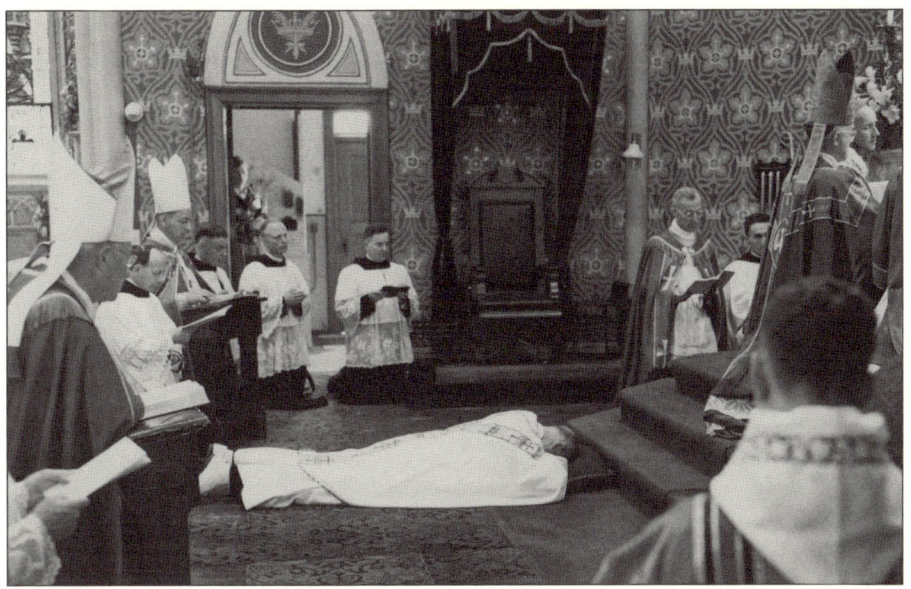

The blessing of Abbot Damian Jentges in St. Mary's Church, Mt. Angel, Oregon, October 5, 1950.

The abbey church, looking into the sanctuary from the nave. The nave area was added in 1950–1952.

1950–1974

The fourth station of the mosaic Stations of the Cross done by Louisa Jenkins for the crypt chapel. The stations were blessed on July 19, 1953.

Taken in the back garden of the monastery after the solemn vows of Fathers Leo Rimele and Augustine DeNoble, September 8, 1953.

A slight accident at the chicken house. Prior Jerome was felling a tree, but the wind was against him.

1950–1974

Laity Day at the abbey hilltop was held once a year on a Sunday in May, in the early 1950s.

Fr. Bernard Sander, who came from Tillamook to be a seminary student. He was in the seminary administration for over twenty-five years and was appointed abbey guest master after that.

Fr. Ambrose Zenner. After earning his doctorate in theology at the University of Fribourg in Switzerland, he worked in seminary administration. He was the first prior of the Cuernavaca foundation. Later he was pastor at Tillamook until his death in a car accident, in 1976.

1950–1974

The construction of Anselm Hall, spring, 1954.

Archbishop Howard blesses Anselm Hall, October 3, 1954. Fr. Leo Rimmele carries the cross; Fathers Patrick Meagher and Sebastian Terhaar accompany the Archbishop.

After the Mass for the 75th Anniversary of Mount Angel Abbey, on October 27, 1957, in front of St. Mary Church, in Mt. Angel.

1950–1974

The abbey dining rooms, 1955. Fr. Boniface Lautz is in the foreground.

The second water tank being assembled in 1959. The operation was directed by Fr. Stephen Hofmann.

Archbishop Howard and Abbot Damian at John F. Kennedy High School in Mt. Angel for its dedication on August 23, 1959. The mosaic in the background was the work of Fr. Dennis Marx.

1950–1974

The newly completed Abbey Retreat House, about 1960.

Abbot Leonard of Engelberg visits Mt. Angel on April 14, 1961. He was the first abbot of Engelberg to visit the Oregon Foundation.

Profession of Brother Simon Hepner, September 8, 1972.

1950–1974

The Columbus Day storm of October 12, 1962.

Then Father Peter Eberle baling hops in his younger days. Hop baling was a regular late August job for the juniors until the hop farm was leased out, in 1976.

The general chapter of the Swiss American Congregation held at Mt. Angel in 1961. The first abbot on the left in the second row is Abbot Anselm Coppersmith of Conception Abbey. Abbot Eugene Medved of Mt. Angel's foundation Westminster Abbey in British Columbia is third from the left in the second row. Abbot Damian is in the lower left corner.

1950–1974

Abbot Damian and Prior Martin Pollard preside over the abbey dining room.

Fr. Albert Bauman (at the left) was the Editor of the St. Joseph Magazine, a weekly national Catholic publication of Mount Angel Abbey. Here he is in 1959 receiving an award for "Best Editorial" from the Catholic Press Association.

Fr. Ambrose (right) shakes hands with his brother, Fr. Edward Zenner, a priest of Archdiocese of Portland, before setting out for Cuernavaca, Morelos, Mexico in a donated bus. Fr. Ambrose was the founding prior, in 1966.

1950–1974

Abbot Damian Jentges, in the 1960s, in front of the Retreat House, which was constructed with his guidance.

Exterior view of the swimming pool, showing sun deck on south side.

1950–1974

Dedication of the swimming pool in 1968.

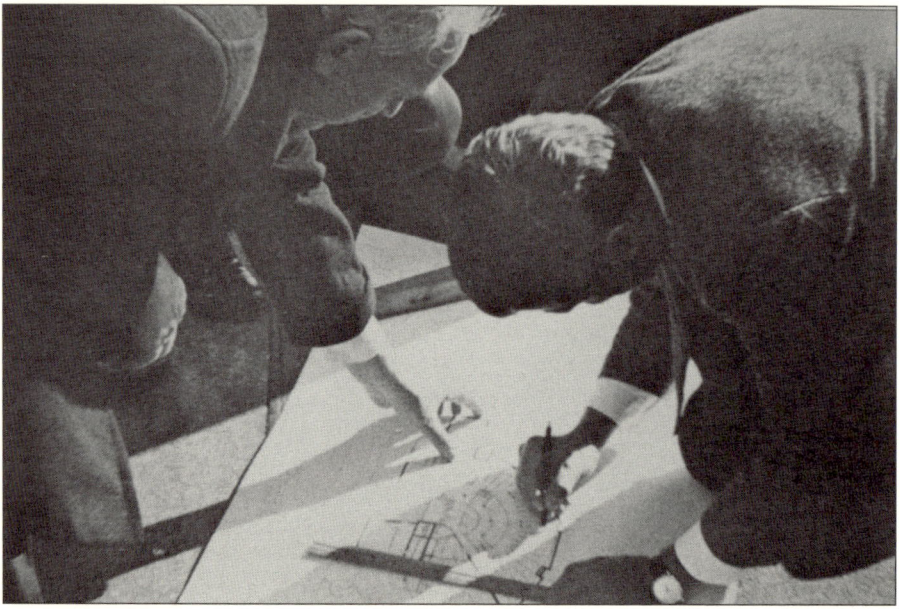

Alvar Aalto and an assistant make changes on the library plans during his only visit to the abbey on April 21, 1967.

1950–1974

Archbishop Robert Dwyer and Abbot Damian look at a scale model of the library.

An aerial view of the newly completed Abbey Library, about 1970.

Pope Paul VI received Abbot Damian, 1973.

1974–1982

hen the community met on October 8, 1974, to elect a successor to Abbot Damian, for many of the electors it was their first abbatial election. They chose as their leader Father Anselm Galvin (deceased 1994) who had been prior since 1971 and had held positions of authority for almost all his monastic life. Abbot Anselm was born in Saskatoon, Saskatchewan, grew up in LaGrande, Oregon, and received his M.A. in English from the University of Toronto. He served in the office of abbot for six years and was succeeded in 1980 by Father Bonaventure Zerr (deceased 1988), who had done doctoral studies in Munich for six years and was professor of Scripture in the seminary and subprior at the time of his election. Abbot Bonaventure had grown up in Sacred Heart parish in Portland, which the abbey had staffed since before the turn of the century.

Abbot Anselm and Abbot Bonaventure were both professors in the seminary. Both were talented preachers and writers, though neither was inclined to seek the public eye. As abbots they had dealt with many of the same matters, so the story of Mount Angel Abbey from 1974 to the present can be combined into a single narrative. The story centers on financial organization, the seminary, the priories, the library and the apostolate of hospitality.

Since 1974, bookkeeping and auditing practices have been improved and a thorough budgeting system has been installed. Investments have been entrusted to an outside firm and an annual report has been issued. A development office has been instituted. The first beginnings of an endowment program have been undertaken. In 1980 Father Andrew Baumgartner returned from Ascension Priory to fill the new post of manager of the business and procurator's office.

Because of changes in the federal tax laws and also because of gradual changes in the makeup of the abbey community, under Abbot Anselm the decision was made to lease out the abbey farm and timber lands. However, the community was determined to keep ownership and to exercise ultimate stewardship of the lands which their Swiss pioneer predecessors laboriously purchased and tamed, and which their successors kept even during the dark days following the two fires. The quality of that stewardship of the place where the community lives will always be an important concern.

The fifteen years following 1965 were a tumultuous time for seminaries. The seminary at Mount Angel switched from minor and major divisions of six years each to a high school, college and theology format. At first each division had its own rector; then the office of president-rector of the entire seminary was established. After 1972 this office was held by diocesan priests: Father (later Archbishop) Elden Curtiss (1972–1976) and Monsignor James Ribble (1976–1982). A number of administrative structures were tried. Three new bodies established during the period were the board of regents, representing the dioceses and religious orders with students in the seminary; a board of lay advisors; and a policy-setting governing board made up of the abbot and nine monks elected by the abbey chapter.

New programs were launched by the seminary. Begun in 1973, a summer school program served the needs of over five hundred students before graduating its final class in July, 1981. The college faculty devised a core curriculum in humanities, which emphasized reading and discussion of primary sources and provided a Christian view of the unity and development of Western culture. The interterm program provided a time for learning opportunities not otherwise available. The graduate school instituted a program of supervised pastoral formation and began to offer accredited M.A., M. Div. and M.T.S. degrees both to seminarians and lay people. A Hispanic ministries program was developed, and its first full-time director joined the faculty in September, 1981. A new pre-theology program was inaugurated for older students entering seminary, to help their intellectual and personal transition to graduate theological studies.

New programs were not the only significant happenings in the seminary. There were years of painful searching for a formation program which would meet the needs of seminarians preparing for the ministry in the Church today. In 1979 the high school division of the seminary ended ninety years of existence, a casualty of declining enrollment, dwindling personnel, and rising costs.

Throughout the period there were countless committees and meetings in the abbey and seminary; some of these achieved tangible results, others did not. Whatever their results, these committees and meetings were evidence of the community's commitment to mutual listening in the joint effort to seek the will of God.

After ten years in Twin Falls, the Ascension priory community under the supervision of Father Stephen Hofmann (deceased 2008) began work on a new monastery complex on their farm near Jerome, Idaho. Designed for twelve monks, the new building looks out over the panorama of Magic Valley. It was blessed by Bishop Nicolas Walsh, long a friend and benefactor of the priory on August 3, 1980. Bishop Treinen celebrated the Mass for the occasion. Shortly before, Father Simeon Van de Voord (deceased 2007) was appointed prior.

At the priory of Our Lady of the Angels in Cuernavaca, Father Louis Charvet (deceased 2007) succeeded Brother Boniface as superior in 1980. He and the community began working to enhance their apostolate of hospitality, their formation program, and their finances, in order to prepare for the day when the priory would become an independent monastery.

Before his election Abbot Bonaventure had been acquisitions librarian. Under his direction the library holdings grew in size and quality. Archbishop Dwyer and William R. Duggan both bequeathed outstanding collections to the library. A printed catalogue of the library's pre-1800 imprints was prepared. In 1981 a computer terminal was installed, and the tens of thousands of books stored in the lowest floor of the library were sorted and prepared for cataloging. The library is steadily becoming a more valuable center for study and research.

In 1980, to commemorate the fifteen hundredth anniversary of the birth of St. Benedict, an exhibit of Aalto's architecture and furniture was displayed on the mall. Mrs. Alvar Aalto and Mr. and Mrs. Howard Vollum visited the abbey during the exhibit, which was arranged largely through the efforts of Father Edmund Smith (professed 1959, prior 1975–1980).

By the mid 1970s the guest-retreat house needed alterations in order to be a more suitable center for the community's hospitality. Father Bernard Sander, the guest-master, catalyzed the planning and secured the initial financing for this remodeling. In July, 1981, the community discussed the addition of a chapel, a conference and meeting level, and improvements in the dining and lounge areas. These were completed in the summer of 1982. Through these renovations Benet Hall was to become a more adequate place for guests, retreats, classes, meetings, and spiritual guidance.

The abbey began its second century of existence with another serious fire, which destroyed part of the gymnasium in May, 1982. The renovated building, christened the Damian Center, was redesigned as a modern gymnasium and music facility. Through the contributions of generous benefactors the hilltop has a more adequate space for athletics and a new home for the Abbey Bach Festival and other events.

In August, 1981, the general chapter of the Swiss-American Federation met at Mount Angel and celebrated 100 years of existence. Over thirty abbots, priors and delegates attended the meeting. They stayed in Benet Hall, which for the occasion flew the American and Swiss flags.

The remodeled conference level of Benet Hall.

As the abbey entered its one hundredth year, there were many signs of vitality: twenty postulants, novices and junior monks; three young monks in Europe studying for advanced degrees; new guest-retreat facilities; an expanding library; a seminary which has shown striking resilience.

There are areas where these vital forces of the community will be stretched to their limit: staffing the seminary with qualified and dedicated teachers and administrators, developing liturgical forms to enhance the prayer of the community, improving skills in communication and decision-making, helping the priories in Idaho and Cuernavaca to independence, renovating the seminary and abbey buildings, discerning what needs of the church the community can best serve.

The first hundred years of the abbey's history, like the centuries of Engelberg's history, suggest that these challenges which loom ahead and the ones which are not yet in sight will be met, and that "as we progress in this way of life and in faith, we shall run on the path of God's commandments, our hearts overflowing with the inexpressible delight of love. Never swerving from his instructions, then, but faithfully observing his teaching in the monastery until death, we shall through patience share the sufferings of Christ, that we may deserve also to share in his kingdom." (Prologue to the *Rule of Benedict*).

Among the effects of titular Abbot Adelhelm, the founder of the abbey, was a letter from Homer Davenport, a renowned cartoonist and story teller, who was born in the Silverton hills. Mr. Davenport related that his father had found some stone seats on the top of the butte where the abbey is now located. Indians told the elder Mr. Davenport that their ancestors had built these chairs as places where they communed with the Great Spirit. "Joe Hutchins, an Indian, said the name of the Butte was Tap-a-Lam-a-Ho, meaning 'The Mount of Communion.'... You call it Mount Angel, and you are building upon it a more costly and elaborate structure than the stone chairs of the natives, but its purpose will ever be the same; and Tap-a-Lam-a-Ho will continue to be the Mount of Communion and prayer for unknown ages."

1974–1982

The chapter members (life-professed monks) of the community during the election of Abbot Anselm Galvin on October 8, 1974.

Abbot Anselm receiving the abbatial ring from Archbishop Cornelius Power at the abbatial blessing on November 26, 1974.

Abbot Anselm's blessing was a historic occasion because three archbishops of Portland were present: Archbishops Dwyer, Howard, and Power.

1974–1982

Monks and Sisters from the Queen of Angels Priory sing at the Parish Centennial Celebration held in honor of the Benedictines in 1979.

Vespers for the sesquimillenium of the birth of St. Benedict on the feast of his passing, March 21, 1980. Abbot Anselm was the celebrant for this opening of the sesquimillenial year.

Vespers for the sesquimillenim (1500th anniversary) of the birth of St. Benedict on the feast of his passing, March 21, 1980. The "1882 – 1982" banner indicates that the community was already anticipating the celebration of the centennial of the Abbey.

1974–1982

Immediately after Abbot Bonaventure's election on June 6, 1980. Left to right: Abbot Raphael DeSalvo, Abbot President of the Swiss-American Federation, who presided at the election; Abbot Bonaventure Zerr and Abbot Anselm Galvin.

The entire community immediately following the election of Abbot Bonaventure, June 6, 1980.

The new buildings for Ascension Priory in Jerome, Idaho.

1974–1982

A variety of scenes (from a post card) of the newly-constructed monastery building at the Monastery of the Ascension, near Jerome, Idaho. The Ascension community, which was established in 1965, was the second daughter house of Mount Angel Abbey.

A photo, taken in the late 1960s, of community of monks at Nuestra Señora de Los Angeles (Our Lady of the Angeles) Cuernavaca, Morelos, Mexico, located about 1 hour by car south of Mexico City. The community was founded in 1966 the third daughter house of Mount Angel Abbey.

The chapel for the monks at Cuernavaca.

1974–1982

The monastery and its setting near Cuernavaca, Morelos, Mexico.

Elisa Aalto, with Abbot Bonaventure, cutting the ribbon at the opening ceremony of the 1980 display which honored the architectural work of her husband, Alvar Aalto.

Abbot Bonaventure receives the crosier from Archbishop Cornelius Power at the abbatial blessing on August 28, 1980.

1974–1982

Abbot Bonaventure Zerr with his mother (left) and sister (right) at the reception after his blessing as abbot. His sister is also a Benedictine, Sr. Jerome Zerr, OSB, of Queen of Angels Monastery, in Mt. Angel.

Delegates gathered for the General Chapter of the Swiss-American Federation in the summer of 1981 and special guest Archbishop Augustine Mayer, O.S.B.

1974–1982

Fr. Hugh Feiss teaching in the seminary college.

Mr. John Degnin in the Development Office.

Br. Benedict Eberle in the Guest House Gift Shop.

1974–1982

Fr. Prior Peter Eberle in his office.

Fr. Paschal Cheline speaks with a junior monk.

Novice Jeffrey Wemhoff in the Abbey Church.

1974–1982

This altar and configuration was used in the Abbey church through the 1970s.

On February 21, 1982, Abbot Bonaventure blessed the new altar in the renovated sanctuary. This is the first stage in the renovation of the church which simplified the area according to the recent liturgical directives and allowed the architecture of the building to show more clearly.

Aerial view of Mount Angel Abbey in the 1980s.

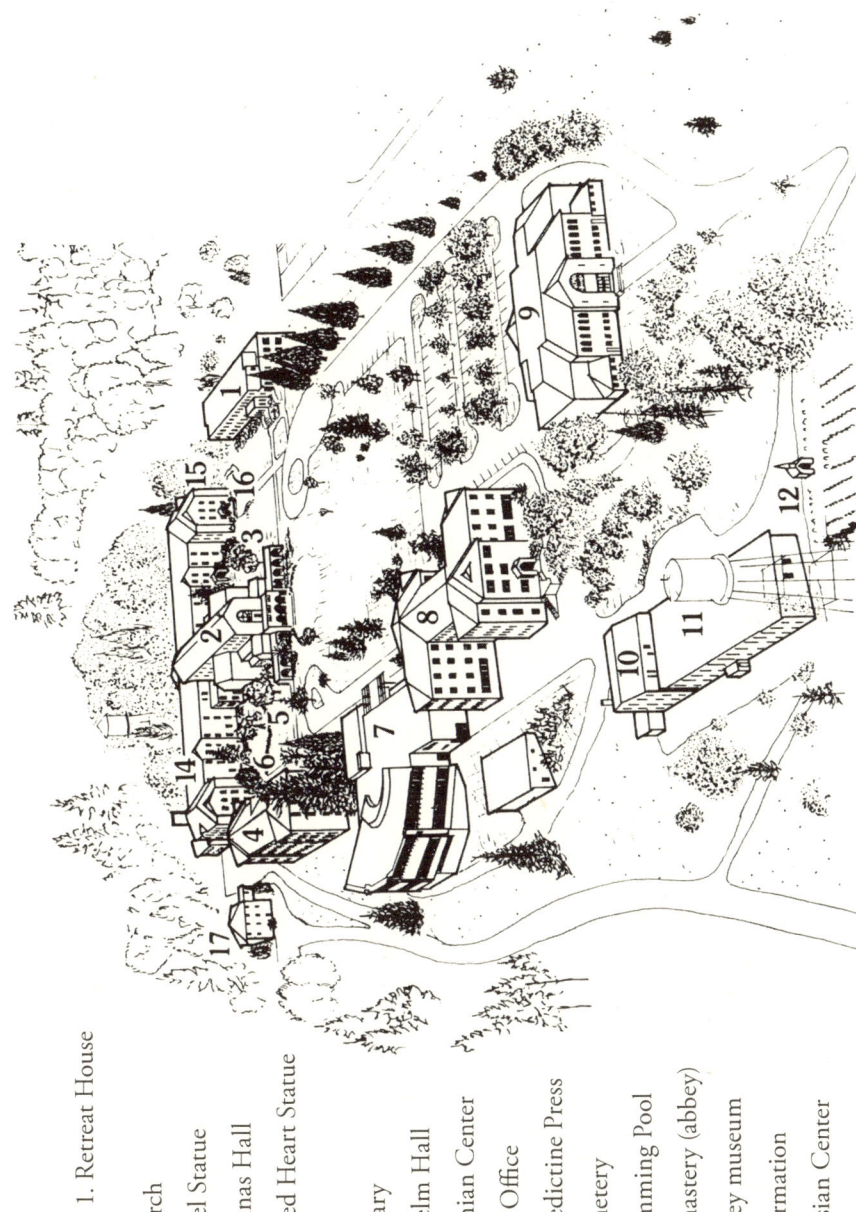

1. Retreat House
2. Church
3. Angel Statue
4. Aquinas Hall
5. Sacred Heart Statue
6. Bells
7. Library
8. Anselm Hall
9. Damian Center
10. Post Office
11. Benedictine Press
12. Cemetery
13. Swimming Pool
14. Monastery (abbey)
15. Abbey museum
16. Information
17. Russian Center

Historical Summary of Mount Angel Abbey

Superiors	Number of Members	Significant Happenings
Prior Adelhelm Odermatt (1882–94)	1882 10	1882 Divine Office Begins at Gervais 1884 First Monastery Building Occupied 1887 First School Opened 1892 Fire Destroys First Monastery
Prior Benedict Gottwald (1894–99) Prior Adelhelm (1899–1901) Prior Thomas Meienhofer (1901–04)	1898 57 1901 56	1899 Indian Missions Begun on Vancouver Island 1902 Mount Angel Joins Swiss-American Federation
Abbot Thomas Meienhofer (1904–10) Prior Adelhelm (1904–16) Abbot Placidus Fuerst (1910–21)		1903 New Monastery on Hilltop Occupied 1904 Mount Angel Becomes an Abbey 1909 New Press Building Built
Prior Maurus Schnyder (1916–21)	1912 67	1916 Father Adelhelm Made Titular Abbot 1914 Post Office Building Constructed
Abbot Bernard Murphy (1921–34) Prior Jerome Wespe (1921–44)	1922 76	1920 Retreats Begun for Lay Persons 1926 Fire Destroys Second Monastery 1928 Present Monastery Occupied 1930 Aquinas Hall Constructed
Abbot Thomas Meier (1934–50)	1932 80	1936 Gymnasium–Auditorium Constructed 1939 Westminster Abbey in British Columbia Founded
Prior James Koessler (1944–46) Prior Martin Pollard (1946–71) Abbot Damian Jentges (1950–74)	1942 84	1946 Athletic Field Constructed 1947 Lay College Closed
	1952 94	1952 Abbey Church and Crypt Completed 1954 Anselm Hall Constructed 1959 John F. Kennedy High School Constructed 1960 Guest–Retreat House Constructed
Prior Anselm Galvin (1971–74)	1962 113	1965 Ascension Priory Founded in Idaho 1966 Our Lady of the Angels Priory Founded in Mexico 1970 Library Dedicated
Abbot Anselm Galvin (1974–80) Prior Edmund Smith (1975–80) Abbot Bonaventure Zerr (1980–1988) Prior Peter Eberle (1980–1988)	1972 113 1982 120	1972 Bach Festival begun 1979 High School closed 1980 New Monastery Dedicated at Ascension Priory